Dietrich BONHOEFFER

The Teacher Who Became a Spy

narrated by
Shep the Sheepdog

Molly Frye Wilmington

illustrated by Marcin Piwowarski

B&H kids
Brentwood TN

To my family, Luke, Kitty, Peggy, Debra, Howard, and especially Anna Grace, who reread this story the most, and David, who helped me find Shep's voice. And in memory of my father, US Army Major John Mason Frye Sr., and my grandfather, US Army Private William August "Bill" Punessen, who fought evil and protected freedom.

Solve the Secret Code!

Solve a secret code like the ones Bonhoeffer used! Starting on the book's last page, search for a dot underneath one letter on some pages. Write the letters down in order as you find them. Read the message and check your answer below.

Answer: STAND FIRM

Hello!

My name is Shep the sheepdog, and I have a tale for you. No, not a dog's tail—a story about a brave teacher who became a spy and fought one of the biggest bad guys of all time.

This is the story of Dietrich Bonhoeffer.

Say his name like this: DEE-trick BON-hoff-er.

Bonhoeffer lived in Germany many years ago. After a terrible war, many Germans were fooled by a new leader, Adolf Hitler. He wanted Germany to be big and powerful, and he was willing to do anything to get what he wanted. He was like a sneaky wolf, and Bonhoeffer knew it.

Bonhoeffer would warn people and rely on God to guide him. You see, Bonhoeffer was like a sheepdog (like me!). Sheepdogs are excellent at herding and protecting sheep because they are smart and follow their shepherds' commands.

Bonhoeffer followed the best shepherd of all, Jesus.

Bonhoeffer was a teacher and pastor who lived in cities worldwide: Barcelona, Berlin, New York City, London, and Finkenwalde (FEENK-in-vohl-derh). He delighted students by telling them about God and the church.

NEW YORK CITY →

SWING LOW, SWEET CHARIOT...

Try saying **Finkenwalde** three times really fast!

He prayed and sang with them, took them on trips to the woods and beach, and was always up for a game.

Bonhoeffer showed his students the Good Shepherd's love. He visited them at home and in the hospital. Some were poor, so he gave them Christmas gifts and bought fabric for fifty students to make new suits. They wore these on the special day they joined the church.

Although Bonhoeffer was a thoughtful and quiet man, he did like clever jokes. While working in Spain, he mailed a postcard to a family member and wrote,

"With greetings from the matador."

He had glued a picture of his own face over the bullfighter's face!

Bonhoeffer often gathered teachers and students to play music and games. One evening, a friend asked Bonhoeffer to join him in a piano duet, but Bonhoeffer tricked his friend by playing the notes in the wrong key, followed by a hearty laugh.

HA HA!

Another evening, one of Bonhoeffer's adult students tried to surprise him by hiding under the piano. But Bonhoeffer didn't know and went to bed. He was surprised the next morning when he found the student asleep and snoring under the piano!

Zzzzz.....

"FREE SOUP AND BREAD"

While Bonhoeffer continued to lead and teach his students, Hitler gained more power. Teachers and pastors often know when someone is not telling the truth. Hitler pretended to follow God and to care about helping people. Many Germans couldn't buy clothes or enough food for their families, and they wanted to believe Hitler would make their country strong again.

At first Hitler helped them, but then he blamed their problems on other countries and, especially, on Jewish people.

Some of Bonhoeffer's friends and family were Jewish, and several of his friends were leaders in other countries. So Bonhoeffer knew Hitler was a liar.

> Jesus was a Jewish man—and is also the Son of God! He fulfills God's promise and brings everlasting life to all who follow Him.

Bonhoeffer saw how that cruel wolf Hitler was leading people away from God. Like the Bible prophets (and sheepdogs!), Bonhoeffer began to warn people of danger.

He spoke on the radio,

STAND FIRM!

wrote **newspaper** articles,

and gave **speeches**.

Sadly, Hitler was elected as the leader of Germany, and his new government—called the Nazis (NOT-zees)—made hundreds of unfair laws. Right away, he declared that Nazis could spy on Germans by reading their mail, listening to their phone conversations, and searching their homes. People were put in prison if they were caught trying to stop the Nazis. This oppression lasted twelve years.

Another law forced Jewish people to sew a special yellow star on their clothes, and the Nazis began putting them in horrible prisons.

Hitler wanted even more power, so he attacked countries nearby. Other countries joined together to stop Germany. This started a massive war called World War 2.

Bonhoeffer needed a way to stop Hitler and protect others, especially the Jewish people. So, like the clever sheepdog he was,

he became a spy!

The Nazis thought Bonhoeffer was using his work as a pastor and teacher to spy *for* them. But for two years, Bonhoeffer spied *on* them and shared news with leaders of other countries.

> *Bonhoeffer knew being a spy was the best way for him to follow God's two greatest commandments— to love God and love your neighbor.*

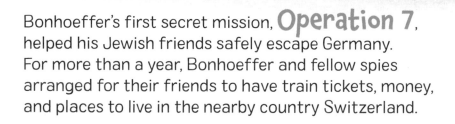

Bonhoeffer's first secret mission, **Operation 7**, helped his Jewish friends safely escape Germany. For more than a year, Bonhoeffer and fellow spies arranged for their friends to have train tickets, money, and places to live in the nearby country Switzerland.

Their bold and dangerous plan saved the lives of these Jewish refugees.

The mission was called Operation 7 to rescue seven people. But more than fourteen were saved!

Another secret mission took Bonhoeffer to the country of Norway. Germany had invaded and had tried to make the churches follow Nazi ideas. The Nazis forced one pastor to leave his church, so Norway's other pastors refused to work. One of their leaders was even taken to prison.

The Nazis sent Bonhoeffer to gather information on the pastors. Instead, Bonhoeffer encouraged the leaders not to give in to the demands of the Nazis.

It worked! The pastors won, and the leader was released.

But Bonhoeffer didn't get much time to celebrate. The Nazis soon found out about Operation 7. They arrested Bonhoeffer and other spies and drove them straight to prison.

STANDING FIRM IN ONE SPIRIT. —PHILIPPIANS 1:27

Still, Bonhoeffer was clever like a sheepdog. He and his family shared secret messages by passing books between the prison and the family at home. If someone underlined Bonhoeffer's name in the front of the book, that meant it held **a hidden code.**

On certain pages, Bonhoeffer or his family used a pencil to make a tiny dot under one letter. The message would start from the back of the book and move toward the front. When the letters were read in order, the secret message was revealed!

Bonhoeffer's nieces and nephews helped find the coded messages. The children could see the tiny dots better than the adults.

Bonhoeffer's family had another surprising spy trick—homemade jelly! They sent him jars of jelly, each with two thin lids pressed together. Between those lids, they hid war updates and plans to stop Hitler.

By passing these secret messages, Bonhoeffer's family—including his nieces and nephews—helped as spies too!

Bonhoeffer also sent codes with made-up stories to other captured spies, who repeated the same stories, tricking the Nazis and protecting many lives.

SPY TRICK

Some prison guards snuck letters from Bonhoeffer to his family and closest friends. Bonhoeffer wrote often to his close friend Eberhard (EH-ber-hard), who also married Bonhoeffer's niece Renate (Reh-NAH-tah). Renate knew a

great sheepdog trick—

she hid Bonhoeffer's letters by burying them inside a sealed container in the backyard.

When the war ended, Renate dug up the container. People still read these letters today!

Bonhoeffer felt sad and lonely in prison. He found courage by reading the Bible and praying. Like a sheepdog who directs the sheep to follow the shepherd, Bonhoeffer found ways to encourage prisoners to follow God.

He passed secret notes with Bible verses, shared the little food he had with those who were sick, and even snuck into another prisoner's cell to pray with him.

Psalm 23 in the Bible reminds us the Lord is our Shepherd who provides comfort and rest and leads us through hard times.

Bonhoeffer hoped he would soon be set free and was even planning to marry his fiancée, Maria.

But tragically all his plans came to an end. German police discovered letters, movies, and photos that the spies had collected as proof of the Nazis' evil actions.

The Nazis questioned Bonhoeffer and the other spies for many more months. Finally, Hitler's army began to lose. Hitler was furious and ordered the death of many prisoners.

Bonhoeffer died on April 9, 1945, after two years in prison. Three weeks later, Hitler died, and within seven days the war with Germany ended.